Boating Fun

by Linda Lott

Scott Foresman
is an imprint of

PEARSON

Glenview, Illinois • Boston, Massachusetts • Mesa, Arizona
Shoreview, Minnesota • Upper Saddle River, New Jersey

Look at the boats in the picture. Which boat is the fastest? Two of the boats were invented long ago. They need people or wind to make them move.

The third boat has a motor. It is faster than the other boats. Motors make riding in boats more **convenient**. People can travel farther and faster in boats with motors. People can use a boat with a motor to move things from place to place without working so hard. These fast boats can be fun too! How can you have fun with these boats?

Water Skiing

Water **skiing** is one way to enjoy a motorboat. Ralph Samuelson was the inventor of the first water skis. He lived in Minnesota in the 1920s. Minnesota has cold winters, and many people there ski on snow. Minnesota also has warm summers and lots of lakes. Samuelson's idea for water skiing helped people have fun in the summer.

This woman is snow skiing.

This man is water skiing.

What You Need to Water Ski

You need a few special things to water ski. First, you need skis. Water skis have special places for your feet so that they will stay on when you are riding. There are many different types of water skis.

Second, you'll need a life jacket. A life jacket will keep you safe if you fall into the water.

Third, you'll need a long rope so that the boat can pull you. It has a handle to hold onto.

Next, you'll need a fast boat with a good driver. A good driver doesn't go too fast or turn too quickly. A good driver will make it easier for you to ride the skis.

Last, you'll need a watcher. While the driver is avoiding other boats, the watcher lets the driver know if you fall down. Then the driver will quickly turn around to get you. Be sure to have at least one adult with you if you go water skiing.

Water skiing has **developed** into a sport for people of all ages. Most people ski for fun. Some people enter contests. Some people can jump or do tricks on skis. You don't have to be grown up to enter a water skiing contest. There are special contests for girls and boys under the age of nine.

Tubing

Water skiing takes practice. There's another way to enjoy skimming over the water. You need an inner tube and a life jacket. The tube is shaped like a doughnut. It is attached to the boat by a rope. The tuber lies down and holds on to the handles on the sides of the tube. When the boat goes, the tuber rides along behind it.

The speed of the boat pulls the tube on top of the water. Because tubers don't stand up, they don't have to worry as much about tipping over. Tubers still must hold on to the tube.

Flying Like a Kite

Another way you can have fun with a boat is by using it to fly! A boat with a motor can pull you like you pull a kite in the air.

To fly a kite, you need speed. When you run with a kite, the kite goes up. The faster you run, the higher the kite goes. When you slow down, the kite comes back down to the ground.

You can ride in a large kite. This large kite is called a **parasail**. First you strap yourself into the seat. Then the boat starts to move. As the boat goes faster, you go up into the air.

You fly through the air. You look down at the boat or people swimming. Now you know how a bird feels.

After you fly for a while, the boat slows down. You come down slowly.

Riding a parasail isn't hard. You don't need to be strong or fast to enjoy it. You don't have to worry about tipping over or holding on. The boat and the driver do all the work. The rider can just sit back and enjoy the view. Sometimes more than one person can fly at the same time! Always be sure there is an adult with you.

Boats have always had a useful **purpose**. They have helped people travel. They have helped people work. Today boats can be used for fun too.

If you are a sailor, you can let the wind push your boat. If you want to go really fast, you need a boat with a motor. Fast boats can pull you on the water and help you fly in the air! Will you join in on the fun?

Boats are convenient and useful for people who live and work near water. Over the years, people have found lots of ways to have fun with boats too.

You've learned about some exciting sports. Now it's your turn to teach a friend what you have learned.

1. Review the different water sports you read about.

2. Choose one that looks fun to you.

3. Draw a picture of someone doing that sport.

4. Add labels to the picture.

5. Use the picture to explain the water sport to a partner.

Glossary

convenient *adj.* easy to use or saving trouble

developed *v.* changed to become bigger or better

parasail *n.* a large sail that lifts people up in the air when pulled behind a boat

purpose *n.* a reason for something

skiing *n.* gliding over snow or water on skis